From the Mouth of Madness

Kayla Chapman

Presentation by *BookLeaf Publishing*

Web: www.bookleafpub.com

E-mail: info@bookleafpub.com

ISBN: 9789395620956

First edition 2022

DEDICATION

I dedicate this to my husband, Rob, who chose me despite my madness.

I also dedicate this to anyone and everyone who has supported and encouraged me through the journey of my life.

Tick tick tick [Tock]

Tick tick tick tock
Time whirls on
Nothing stops the break of dawn
Woken too soon
By deafening call
Alarm clock rings from down the hall
Tick tick tock
Another bell
It's the postman
Ain't he swell?
Brown paper package
Tied with a string
At six in the morning
Not my favorite thing
Tick tock
Coffee pot
Paper boy
Scrubby dub
Out the door
Traffic Jam
Stop.
I've forgotten my breakfast.

Trinity

Come now sweet child
Don't cry
Mommas here to hold you

Boogeyman and monsters
Under the bed
Mommas here now, don't you cry

My hopes and dreams come to life
In your beautiful blue eyes
In you I see everything
I love about your father, and the world

Hush sweet baby
Don't you cry
Everything will be alright
It's us against the world
And we're winning

Dark Colors

Darkness comes in
and fills us with fright
Can't cover it up
Unless you will fight
Black dances in
Gaiety born
The guests at the party
Start to look forlorn

Oh these dark colors
Bearers of the night
Oh these dark colors
They fill us with fright

Darkness comes towards
Dances with a guest
Black dances forewards
And handles the rest
The guest begins dancing
The colors are gay
Black is romancing
Darkness flies away

Oh these dark colors
How sweet, and so gay

Only thing that can break them
The light of the day

Black keeps on dancing
And spinning
And prancing
Darkness takes leave
As the day starts to break
Black doesn't see this
As it tries to take
Another swing at the guest
Who is drawn by a light
The daylight
Sweet daylight
Black soon fades away
and the colors all lighten
To the colors of day

Love

Life it seems never stays the same
Another year goes by
Names and faces quickly change
And time just flies on by

Here I am, the same old me
My life, though, how it's changed
Everything I once believed
Has completely rearranged

If you had told me years ago
That these things would be true
That I would love and lose and find
Someone as swell as you

I'd have laughed right in your face
And said not me, not I
For so long I believed
I'd be alone until I'd die

Somewhere along my lonesome way
A friend became my love
And now it seems so heaven sent
A gift from above

As life changes we grow old
But never grow apart
It seems I've found the other half
Of my ever lonely heart

A Picture of Us

Fake smiles, plastered on
Blissfully oblivious to the world around
Forgetting that there are problems bigger
than the ones in the foreground

Taciturn soldiers, marching to a catastrophic
beat
We continue on our road of blissful solitude
Alone
Enveloped in ourselves despite false pretensions
Of sympathy
Of love
Of emotions that once made us human

Pills to make us happy
Painting on our faces, pretending to be beautiful
Diamonds are forever
Click goes the camera
Upload to Facebook
We're all exactly the same

Everything and Nothing In Between

Locked in the confines of a fragile mind
A young girl cries out for freedom
Freedom from the masses
but fear of rejection
becomes the chain that binds her
Fear of loss
consumes the vast expanses of her mind
And constricts the creativity
That could have saved the world

Fairy Tale

This tower of solitude, with walls of
impenetrable steel
The cold, lonely feeling encompassing me
I sit, and I wait
For someone brave enough to leap these walls
And whisk me away into my fairytale

Clip Clop Clip Clop
Valiant steed, don't stop
My princess awaits
By a monster she's caged

Into the darkness you come,
Sweet prince
To rescue me from the monster that has locked
me in this tower

Sword unsheathed, I rush to my princess
Spinning in circles, searching, searching
Monster?

Immortally beloved, the monster is me
I have kept myself locked up, for so long
Hurt too many times, afraid of the world

My princess, I come
Though the monster is only in your mind
To have and to hold
From this day forward
Never again tossed to the carelessness of a
foolish boy

My prince, I thought this day would never come
The day I would find light in this cruel, dark
place
The day I would truly find my happy ending

Placeholder

Love is Blind
Because of this
This fallacy became truth
Because of this I fell
For you

How was I to know
That I was merely a placeholder
A placeholder, in your heart
For a tear that she created
Because she tore you apart
How was I to know
That we entered with the same intentions
But now, we've reached a divide
A division of hopes
Of dreams
Of trust
Of love...

Originally, you too were a placeholder
Meant only to stay in my heart
While it was on the mend
But then...
Oh then...
The scar that should have been

Was replaced by something new
Something sweet

Since feeling is first
Who pays attention
To sensibility
Common sense
Or your brain

Wishing

Impassioned writer
Dips her pen in blood instead of ink
She pours the sustenance of her heart onto paper
For the world to see
Wishing someday
To be heard

Blind

I have been estranged
From a world which does not know
Which does not see
A world which does not
Will not
[Could not] see
The inner side of me

Into the Sepulcher

Into the sepulcher of my heart, my love
Deep within my chest
There you will find no signs of love
No sign of bloods caress

Into the tomb of sorrow, my love
Where once there used to be
Signs of life, of joy, and hope
And of vitality

Your sacred eyes and wondrous smile
Seem to bless what others taint
While others seem to quickly pass
You march, just like a saint

So into the sepulcher of my heart, my love
Deep within my chest
And you can plant your seed of love
And with your kisses, bless

Into the tomb of sorrow, my love
And with you bring your light
To illuminate the chasm
And bring me back to life

Memory Lane

I took a walk down memory lane
My best friend at my side
And as those memories flooded in
I had to say goodbye
Those silly fights
Those late late nights
Staying up til 5 AM
Oh what I wouldn't give
To live like that again

Foolish Dream

The anger that I once thought I felt
Has decimated to nothing
Nothing but the grief you left me
The sorrow of knowing how you really feel

Although I thought I hated you
I don't and more than ever
I wish it wouldn't have been this way
It shouldn't be this way

The only hate within me now
Is of myself for what I've done
I've ruined so much in so little time
I wonder how I could possibly live on

A friendshp
Maybe two
And the lifetime I thought I'd share
With you

The only anger I feel now
Is at myself
For allowing such a fragile thing
To break like glass before me

The only sorrow I have
Is for myself
For being such a coward
Unable to express my regret but in a poem

The only things I feel
Are for myself
It seems, that's what you think
I don't know if it's true

Young, and mindless love
The love I felt for you
The love you turned against me
The thought that is the truth

Nothing more than a foolish dream
Shattered and tossed aside
To haunt me later
The everlasting memory of your eyes

It leaves me haunted
This foolish dream of mine
The memory of your kiss burned into my mind
My mind's eye forever faltered

Nothing more than a foolish dream
Brought up with false hopes then shot down
The one thing I thought made me happy
Left me worse off than I was before

The tears I've shed
Because of this foolish dream
Were cried in hopes you'd hear me
Cried in hopes of bringing it back to the light

No such thing will ever happen
The foolish dream was torn and shattered
It can not rekindle the feelings
It will only renew the pain

I Can't Write

An endless drama
A plague
A never ending struggle
To put my thoughts to words
But nothing comes

Every time I sit
With pen in hand
Intending to write
Thoughts in my head
But nothing comes

The monotonous cycle
Is completely endless
My creativity
Has come
to an end

No Such Thing As Too Much

Sometimes
When I watch you as you sleep
I wonder
If I can ever feel my love is good enough for you
If I can ever be perfect, if only for you
If I can ever be everything you want, and more
If I can ever make you infinitely happy
Then when you wake
With the sun shining on your face
Your beautiful smile
Your soothing voice telling me
'I love you too much'
and the laughter you cause
Because there is no such thing
As too much.

Better Off

I'm happy with him
I love him, with all of my heart
I'm much better off because we are apart
I'm happy with him
But I don't quite get
Why inside of me seems to be hidden regret
I can't stand thinking of you with her
I can't stand thinking of you at all
It makes my stomach turn to think
Of all the things we did and said
And putting her in my own place
My heart seems to lose it's pace
When I think of how hurt and how lost I once
was
Though I was the one taking blame
For the love we had, now lost
For the heart that I sent down in flames

My regrets lie not in being with him
But for anything I may have caused you
Perhaps it is me who's to blame for it all
For your life hitting such a downward spiral
And if it is, know this
I don't regret leaving you, I regret hurting you

Because in my heart, we are friends

I'm happy with him, you see
I love him, and he loves me
And it grieves me so, to know
That our friendship couldn't be salvaged in spite
of my immaturity and my error
And a heart takes time to mend, I know
And though the process may be slow
I'm happy with him, you're happy with her
We're both so much better without eachother
I'm happy with him, you're happy with her
And for us, I couldn't ask more
We're so much better than before

The Monster Under My Bed

Mommy tucked me in tonight
And my heart was filled with fright
A thing that shows only at night
This terrible, awful, horrendous sight

A gruesome monster under my bed
Who fills my thoughts, controls my head
A gruesome monster, under my bed
Who makes me wish that I was dead

I saw it, last night
This terrible beast
I thought for sure
He would have a feast
On my entrails

I'm nearly afraid to exhale
He creeps and he crawls in the dark
So beastly, so nasty, so awful, so smelly
It's enough to spark
Such fear, such agony....
I'M TOO YOUNG TO DIE

My Life

Here's my life
Set out before you
like an artistic masterpiece

This space is my canvas
These words are my paint
And my muse is the art laid before you

I've been waiting
For these pieces to fall into place
To create such a beautiful piece

I've been waiting
For paint to meet canvas
For so long
So here it is

I give you my heart
I give you my all
Through my writing
Through my art
Through my life

Searching

I walked down the hall
Searching, searching
For answers to life's questions

'Religion'
 I gladly entered, curiosity getting the best of me
Inside, there was nothing
But rows upon rows of books
A church pew, a crucifix, a table with incense
A buddha, a Torah,A Bible, a Q'uran a star of
David

I pondered at what this could mean, I exited the
room
Returned to the hall, walking further and further
Until I came upon the next door, unlabeled
I opened it up and stepped inside
I found pictures from life
From childhood up until adulthood
And there I was on my dying bed
Searching for salvation

I took two steps back
And quickly left, continuing on my pursuit
I knew I had come for something more

Something deeper

I searched and I searched
Through 'Hope', 'Fear', and 'Wisdom'
I glanced through 'Pain' and 'Trust'
I carefully dissected my way through 'Memory'
 I just couldn't find it

I searched for 'Love'
And I couldn't find it
I searched for 'Love'
And it fled my pursuit
Hiding so deftly and keeping away
So my heart
Could never
Be content

She Loves The Fall

She loves the winter
When colors fade to grey
When cold, harsh winds accompany
The brilliant light of day

She loves the winter
When frostbitten toes
Find the fire who knows
Just when to keep them warm

She loves the spring
When the flowers
Come after April's showers
And The cold fades
Into the brilliant colors of day

She loves the spring
When the birds
Sing their songs
That they took all winter long
To learn

She loves the summer
When children are out to play
When the dog lays out to sun himself

As the sprinkle wets the dry lawn
Tsk Tsk Tsking the weather
For drying out the land

She loves the summer
Sleeping in 'til noon
Lazy days and crazy nights
Partying, and silly fights
Working hard for the weekend
And not regretting a thing

But most of all
She loves the fall
When the crisp, clean air
Fills her lungs
When we're all thankful for what we have
And jumping into piles of leaves
Oh, what fun we have

She loves the fall
Turkey and dressing
And football
Kiddies running around dressed as ghosts
And ghouls, with Jack-o-laterns on the porch
Oh yes, she loves the fall

Heartsongs

Although I live in shackles
and my body's bound by chains
I live in peace, without regret
I live within remains

Remains of
A better life
Remains that used to be
devoid of strife

My heart's a bird
Though caged
It will sing
Heartsongs

Heartsongs of peace
Heartsongs of love
Heartsongs of a life
Somewhere above
Heartsongs of a place
Where pictures aren't whats left
Heartsongs of a time
Where a smile isn't hard to find

And oh, these remains

These heartsongs
These pains

Heartsongs of freedom
Heartsongs of flight
Heartsongs of a life
That isn't a fight

Heartsongs of home
Heartsongs of love
Heartsongs of you

www.ingramcontent.com/pod-product-compliance
Lightning Source LLC
LaVergne TN
LVHW021330200726
843509LV00014B/2475